STEPPING

STONES...

Reflections for Singles

Volume 1

Jeri Darby

Ararity Press

Graye,
I pray that God will keep
His Gracious Hand upon
you throughout every season of your life.
He loves you dearly.
Love,
Jeri Darby

Stepping Stones
Reflections for Singles
Volume I
by
Jeri Darby

ISBN-13:978-0692604557 (Ararity Press)
ISBN-10: 0692604553

Ararity Press
Jeri Darby
P.O. Box 5682
Saginaw MI 48603
www.araritypress.com
araritypress@gmail.com
989 717-1031

Dedication

This book is dedicated to:
Jesus Christ, who is the Author and Finisher of my faith.

The Holy Spirit, my Comforter, Counselor, Guide and my
very best Friend.

To the Eternal, Immortal, Invisible and the Only
Wise God, my Heavenly Father who is my Endless Source
and Sustainer.

Acknowledgements

There are so many who cheered me on over the years as I wandered on and off the author's path. Among them my children Jimmie, Johnnie, Desmond and especially my daughter Yolonda who was a steady sounding board and an editor extraordinaire.

Sandy Shepherd whose writer's conference years ago was crucial to my journey and paved the way to years of magazine publications. A special thanks to my dear friends: Sheryln Miller who held my hand and guided me through the self-publishing process— one step at a time. Pastor Patricia Qualls, a gifted writer and a long time divine connection. Minister Debra Smithson; my new divine connection. Minister Rita Truss who watered my gift with words of life during dry seasons. Minister Patricia Hampton whom I could always rely on for fervent prayer.

I'm also grateful to Pam Harris and her red pen who did the final proofreading of Stepping Stones. Sophia Nikoliviavna who assisted with the final phases of the technical process of self-publishing. Lastly, Robert Conner, my massage therapist who help me destress before diving into my solo writing retreats.

Though too numerous to name; I extend a heartfelt thanks to everyone and anyone who continued believing in me. Words cannot give justice to how valuable your encouragement has been. Remember you all vowed to purchase my book once completed. Though it is twenty years later— you may *now* receive your autographed copy! I thank God for each and every one of you and pray that your dreams will also become your realities.

Preface

Jessamyn West said, "You make what seems a simple choice. Choose a man or a job or a neighborhood—and what you have chosen is not a man or a job or a neighborhood, but a life." Reflecting on the unsuccessful marriage of my younger years; the truth of these words blares.

Back then, we were both new Christians and loved God. Matchmakers swarmed—we were among the few young singles in our small congregation. "I had a dream that you two got married... You two make a g-o-o-d couple..." Well-meaners coerced.

"Why not?" We both decided— in haste. Then second thoughts arrested me...

"We shouldn't go through with this!" I blurted to my soon husband-to-be after finally grabbing the courage. Our wedding date was weeks away. God was clearly saying *"NO-OOO!"* I knew His voice and now understand that He was trying to detour me from years of sorrow. It never dawned on me that *if* my husband quit living by Christian standards that he could resume his previous patterns of drug addiction, crime and prison— *but God knew.*

"What will we tell everybody? We al--ready mailed the invitations and everything!"

"Ok! Ok! You're right! We might as well... "I relented—as if his nervous rantings were valid reasons to disobey God and base one of life's *most* important decisions. Those who knew I was making a mistake declined confronting me— including my parents. I think they were hoping I would snap to my senses- I didn't. I discounted subliminal warnings emitted by their eyes and voices. Turns out that attending the same church and being single were the only things we had in common. It takes more to build a successful marriage—*much* more.

Our day arrived and I dragged myself down the aisle feeling like a zombie while my heart juggled many uncertainties. The grief of the Holy Spirit hazed the air like a thick smog. A glimpse of my awaiting fate would have convinced me to turn and race out of that church- no looking back- *no* remorse. We were as mismatched as two left shoes.

Separation and eventually divorce proceeded years of sorrow and disenchantment. Only God's grace sustained me. One thing I gained from this—when God says "no" or "wait," it's *never* too late for a change of heart— *Stop* the wedding!!! Amos 3:3 NIV says, "Can two walk together, unless they are agreed?" The answer is, "*no.*"

You will not find a list of how-tos or formulas for dating success in my book. These writings are merely reflections of my inner thoughts, emotions, experiences, observations; along with conversations with others compiled over the years. I address challenges that are common to many singles who may sometimes need reminders that though we are single— we are *never* alone.

Our lives are preplanned by God Himself.

Every satanic assignment has been

factored in.

Table of Contents

9

10

He Knew

God is not amazed
By your achievements.
He's not confounded
By your problems.
He cannot be intimidated
By your anger.
He's not embarrassed
By your fears.
Your weaknesses are not
Disappointing to Him.
No aspect of your being
Has caught Him off guard
Before creation
All that you were
All that you are
All you'll ever become
He knew…

Future

"Because He lives, I can face to-mo-oro-ow," I sung this hymn written by Bill and Gloria Gaither along with the outreach team. We were ministering to a group of inmates at the local jail. I had recently returned to church and renewed my commitment to the Lord.

I couldn't shake haunting memories of the wasted years, unhealthy relationships and shattered dreams swimming in my head. Though I was glad for my blossoming relationship with God, remorse was my constant companion.

The years ahead looked bleak. I felt I no longer had time to fulfill my aspirations. My dreams had withered and died. These thoughts circulated as I sung. "Be-cause I kno—o-ow He holds my fu—ture..." The song invaded my spirit like a torpedo. I was instantly splattered with renewed faith and vision. God holds my future! My life no matter how broken is in the Master's hand.

The revelation that life could *yet* be fulfilling and exciting was permanently etched in my heart. While I ministered to the inmates, the Holy Spirit was reigniting my hope.

I left no longer grieving past failures that I was powerless to change- but visualizing a future overflowing with limitless possibilities- because *He* lives!

Brethren, I count not myself to have apprehended: but this one thing I do, forgetting those things which are behind, and reaching forth unto those things which are before, I press toward the mark for the prize of the high calling of God in Christ Jesus.
Philippians 3:13, 14 KJV

Burnt

**Love is a fire. But whether it is going to
warm your hearth or burn down your house,
you can never tell.
Joan Crawford**

I love toast! No, not that pop-in–the-toaster with its
pre-calculated heat and safety features. I prefer browning
my toast under the oven's open flames. Well, life's full of
distractions. Pungent odor soon desecrates the atmosphere
and I scramble to salvage it. Too late! Burnt toast—*again!*
Sometimes it's humorous— and I chuckle. Gawking with
disbelief, I toss the charcoal bread and start from scratch.

Luring flames of passion hurl many into impulsive
sexual activities. Practicing the safety features in God's
word can enable us to escape before becoming engulfed.
Sure; I've plunged beneath taunting flames of passion- too
hot from the get-go while ignoring all the precautions. Soon
aromas of my singed emotions circulate signaling burnt
heart— *again!* Let those without singe- cast the first stone.

Nothing's humorous about burnt hearts. Unlike
bread, we only have *one* and it cannot be trashed. Scraping
charred areas from my torched heart was painful and
tedious. "God, will I ever recover?" I asked. I didn't think
I would.

Sometimes I'm lonely, but my heart is *too* valuable
to be entrusted to my fickle emotions. Burnt hearts require
special nurturing, fortunately, God is an expert. Time in His
presence is like aloe vera. Under His compassionate care
and supervision my heart was *fully* restored. He will restore
your burnt heart too- just *ask*.

**Keep your heart with all diligence,
For out of it springs the issues of life…
Proverbs 4:23 NIV**

DeJaVu

Life is change: Growth is optional...
Karen Kaiser Clark

After leaving my marriage; I was spiritually depleted and plagued by loneliness when I began drifting. While separated from church and all sources of spiritual support; I was driven by impulsivity and emotionalism. I embraced yet *another* detrimental relationship! Though clear warnings stared me down I ignored them— again! I know; unbelievable...

Though we never married another ten years of my life whizzed by and I stood mesmerized by the dissipating winds of drugs, disappointment and disaster. Constant storms had whirled through our lives.

God rescued me— *again* from another disastrous relationship. He is so faithful! I praised him as the drama dust in my life began to settle. Our Father, God keeps busy snatching his single daughters and sons off destructive paths that we were never meant to travel.

It is of the Lord's mercy that we are not consumed
Lamentations 3:22 KJV

Abstinence?

Realizing the proper use of sex is the first step toward controlling the sex drive. When you know how God wants you to use the sexuality he gave you, the goal is set.
Lester Sumrall

"God, where do I go from here?" I asked after leaving a second ten-year relationship and returning to Him. A deafening silence followed, Whew! Glad He *didn't* answer! A new relationship was not an *immediate* desire—too wounded; too weary. If God had said, "You will live the next twenty two years single and celibate—" I was *not* prepared for *that* level of truth.

Singles are sometimes reluctant to commit their lives *fully* to God because they feel it's *impossible* to abstain from sex. Controlling the flames of passion imparts discipline and molds character. These attributes pave the way to spiritual maturity—which paves the way to fruitful relationships.

Not always easy—but what is? Is heartache? Are severed unions after indulgence in premature sexual intimacy? Or STD's? Definitely not! Singleness has diverse phases—there are seasons of elation emerging from a sense of immense freedom. There are seasons of incredible spiritual growth, self-discovery, and transformation and yes—even those cloudy seasons when pangs of loneliness feel all too consuming. A genuine desire to honor God with my body sustains me. Abstinence? By His grace— it's doable.

Present your body a living sacrifice, holy and acceptable To God and be not conformed to this world... but be transformed by the renewing of your mind...
Romans 12:1 NIV

Seasons

All things flow, nothing abides.
Heraclitus

After God redeemed me from unhealthy relationships—I surrendered myself *fully* to Him. Two ten-year seasons of detriment wiped me out relationally! Just listening to others express urgent hopes of marriage zapped me with instant nausea.

"I don't care if I *e-ver* get married!" I emphatically proclaimed to a group of singles. "Jesus is all I need— and all I will *e-ver* need." I declared, speaking from my *hurt*. Pain has a voice and mine was screaming.

The matured women assured me that it was only a *season* and would *soon* pass. They consistently shot down my debates. "Right—it'll pass! They just don't understand!" I silently surmised- certain that I was unwilling to risk such pain again— *e-ver!!!*

Guess what? They were right! Just a season! A season of healing. After three years or so— marriage was no longer a four-letter word. Fear of resurrecting and reliving past nightmares were dissipating. God dissolved the bitterness and I anticipated sharing life with a *Christian* partner.

Often singles get stuck in seasons of recycled pain and fear or they skid into a new relationship—*prematurely*. A healing season is *needed* in order to erect a foundation secure enough to build a new, healthy Godly relationship.

To everything there is a season and a
Time for every purpose under heaven…
Ecclesiastes 3:1 KJV

Wonderful

**You come to love not by finding the perfect person,
but by seeing an imperfect person perfectly.
Sam Keen**

"Waiting for the *Perfect* Man," the captioned read. It pictured the skeletal remains of a woman sitting alone on a park bench with a purse in her lap. A spider's web draped her neck like hair flowing from her skull. I made copies of this handout I received at a single's conference.

"Take one." I said handing my co-worker a sheet while passing in the hallway.

"Thanks, Jeri," she said later that day. "This helped me to put things back into perspective. "I am not pleased with that man today!" Her wedding was a year and a half earlier and she had a three-month-old daughter. They seemed happily married.

We laughed as she entered her office. The picture symbolizes what happens when *unrealistic* standards are set for a potential partner. *No one* is perfect.

Embracing impossible standards will *doom* you to singlehood. Though no one is perfect, I believe God has someone wonderful for me—and perfect for you; *if* marriage is your desire. It's not perfection that yields the fruit of a *not perfect-* but wonderful marriage, but two people committed to loving each other —*unconditionally.*

**Every good and perfect gift is from above, coming down
from the Father of the heavenly lights, who does not change
like shifting shadows.
James 1:17 NIV**

Dance!

**Dancing is a very crude attempt to get into
the rhythm of life.
George Bernard Shaw.**

Remember the anticipation rising as the person strolls across the room, looks into your eyes and extends a hand? It's an invitation to dance… Dancing is a form of nonverbal communication. Once the two of you are in sync words are not necessary-it's enthralling!

The best dancers miss a step or plop a toe now and then while praying that nothing's said. They smile and keep on dancing; it's soon obvious-no one cares. Verbal dancing with the opposite sex can be even more challenging.

I receive invitations to engage in verbal dancing. Sometimes I accept. Then it happens. Someone stumbles or misses a beat *(usually me)* - I quickly exit! My partner stands alone, dazed and wondering, "What happened!" I desire to meet a special person and even get married someday. This can only happen if I stop scurrying away at the climax of verbal dancing. It's the joining in conversation and twirling through differences and dipping in and out of each other's life experiences that cultivates the dance of *genuine* friendship.

Friendship is the launching pad for romantic interest. Romantic interest is the launching pad for commitment. Commitment is the launching pad for marriage. I pray for *courage* and keep telling myself- "Don't be a fraidy-cat- Dance!!! Dance!!! Dance!!!!!!!

**I will build you up again, and you, Virgin Israel, will be
rebuilt. Again you will take up your timbrels and go out to
dance with the joyful.
Jeremiah 31:4 NIV**

Help!

"It was scary. I was like, Jesus, Jesus help me."
Nicole Turner

"Look at your neighbor and repeat after me., *Lord, I have no man to help me,"* the congregation chanted this in unison. We had a guest minister that wore out audience participation while delivering his sermon.

I don't often joke during service but; I couldn't resist. I quickly scribbled a note, *"Lord, I have no man, HELP ME!"* I passed it to a friend behind me. Our eyes collided and we trembled with giggles. Moments later a tap on my shoulder grabbed my attention.

She handed back my note with, *"Lord, I have no man and I DON"T WANT HELP"* jotted beneath mine. We chuckled again. A few months ago she glowed in a manner that only a woman in love could. Her relationship fizzled with their wedding plans. Trust in a loving God sustained her, A God who will help when there is no man-or woman to stand in the gap. When the relationship sunk and wedding plans ceased, she clung to God who never fails.

Our help is in the name of the LORD,
who made heaven and earth.
Psalm 124:8 KJV

Recalled

"You have been recalled to life..."
Charles Dickens

I knew a woman whose life began withering when she refused to release a damaging relationship. It literally consumed her life. She was somewhat overweight initially; but by the time she died she was over five-hundred pounds. It was no secret that this man did not love her; yet he had a revolving door in and out of her life at his leisure. The physical and emotional abuse were tell-tell signs that this was *not* a good relationship- but she *always* took him back.

When separated she pleaded relentlessly for his return. He did- on and off for over twenty years only to infuse her life with more abuse and to destroy any remaining residue of a healthy self-image. She died grossly obese, depressed and alone. When your heart aches to be with a particular person, whether the result of separation is death, divorce or desertion; letting go and moving on can be a difficult process.

There is no pain quite like unrequited love. It hurts. The important thing is not to stop in the middle of the recovery process. Pining away for something that will *never* be is not the answer. Neither is opting out of really participating in the art of living- this is not the life that God wants for you. The quote above is taken from Charles Dickens book titled, "A Tale of Two Cities," it is profound. Regardless of the pain, the hurt or the struggle that past relationships have inflicted- *today*; right *now* Jesus is recalling *you* to life.

The thief cometh not, but for to steal, and to kill, and to destroy: I am come that they might have life, and that they might have it more abundantly.
John 10:10 KJV

Rumors

Trust yourself. Your perceptions are often far more accurate than you are willing to believe.
Claudia Black

Against all inner instincts I befriended a man- we were both writers. This ended our commonalities. God knows I had *no* romantic fantasies—*he also knew*. I ignored aspects of his personality that I found atrocious. He attended church with me a few times. When he did eyes locked on us throughout the service. Rumors and gossip erupted like a whale's gushing spout. People made assumptions like people tend to do.

Both Christians and non-Christians are often reluctant to believe that you *are* really *celibate.* Anything supporting unfounded suspicions is eagerly clutched. "I want you to meet him;" I told a close friend whose opinion I valued. The two were invited over for coffee and after just a *few* minutes my friend stood behind him frowning and waving her arms wildly. "No! No! No!" She lip synched and later shared the shady vibes she immediately sensed— the very ones I discounted— couldn't have justified allowing his invasion into my life otherwise.

Loneliness is deceptive and may cause you to tag an undeserving person *"friend"*— when you know better. I severed this relationship; but not before vicious lies were spread about the nature of our friendship—*by him.* Authentic friendships with the opposite sex can be great! Choose wisely...

Let not then your good be evil spoken of:
Romans 14:6 KJV

R-unnnn!!!

We have met the enemy and he is us.
Walt Kelly

We were alone, out of town— I knew better. I harbored strong feelings for him; but his sole objective was to seduce me. No surprise— we *both* knew this. "It's been years since you had sex—no one will ever know," satan taunted.

"Leave!" The Holy Spirit clearly warned. Mesmerized by vibrant language, romantic mood and the pleasure of seductive advances—*I hesitated.* God created my physical body and gifted it with an inborn desire for sex. He knows the relentless force of this drive and the discipline required to subdue it.

"Leave!" The Holy Spirit warned *again*— I ignored—*again.* "If you don't leave *now*—you *won't*," the urgent prompting arose the third and final time. It took all my strength; but I left— in haste. The Bible instructs us to flee from fornication. Flee means- "to run away from a place or situation of danger." (Oxford Dictionary)

I don't know of any other instance where the Bible instructs Christians to *run* as when dealing with sexual cravings. It's not an issue of overpowering the advances of another— but can we overpower the desires erupting from our own flesh? Can we muster the strength needed to even try?

God works— on our behalf and no matter what it looks like; He has *only* our best interest at heart. Obedience—reaps rewards. If He directs— without question, hesitation, rationalization or justification— *r---unnnn!!!*

Flee from sexual immorality…
I Corinthians 6:18 NIV

Ahhhaaa!

"A lot of people get so hung up on what they can't have that they don't think for a second about whether they really want it."
Lionel Shriver

"What do you *want* in a relationship?" A friend questioned during a phone conversation?

"Some—o-n-e, com—pa-ti--ble," I stumbled, struggling for words to dialogue further. My mind blanked. Yet this question nested in my head. I realized that I focused on what I *didn't* want rather than what I wanted.

I knew what I desired in my heart. I wrote this after much mental recycling. "I want a man who is in partnership with God and knows Him not only by the letter of His word, but in the daily maneuverings of his life. Someone willing to stop and pray on a dime and who understands that prayer is not just a sanctimonious religious act, but a *real* way of touching God.

A man who realizes that faith "*can and does*" move mountains and clings to God's promises amidst life's adversities. A man illuminated by a revelation of "*real*" love, because God's love flows through him. A man willing to honor the covenant of marriage and understands that it is not merely a legal and cultural formality; but a *sacred* act before a Living God…"

Though these things are not conclusive; they are foundational. Clarity is liberating! It navigates. My pastor said, "Make up *your* mind what you want-- then walk away from *everything* else…" I agree.

Delight thyself also in the LORD: and he shall give thee the desires of thine heart.
Psalms 37:4 KJV

Wholeness

The single person
Is viewed with pity
By those looking
From without.

But it was through
My singleness
That I discovered,
What living was all about.

The single person
Is viewed as lonely
By married
Women and men.

But through
My singleness,
I have learned,
To be my own best friend.

The single person
Is often viewed
As a half,
Rather than whole.

But through my singleness
I discovered,
A completeness
Worth more than gold.

Preparation

"For one human being to love another; that is perhaps the most difficult of our tasks; the ultimate, the last test and proof; the work for which all other work is but preparation."
Rainer Maria Rilke

Thrust together in our careers demanded that we routinely spend many hours together. Half the time we squabbled, the other half we were not speaking. It is nothing like seeing your flaws mirrored through another. "I'm sorry for the tension growing between us lately." I apologized-*again!* The apprehension had become so thick it was like breathing in smog.

"It's okay" she replied, being genuine and always forgiving. "I told a friend that our work relationship is just preparation for marriage," she continued.

"I shared that same theory with a friend just this week," I said. We laughed. "It's just that I hadn't planned to work this hard on a relationship *until* I got married," I elaborated.

"If I am unable to resolve conflict with someone with whom I spend a portion of my day, how will I face challenges with a person to whom I vow to share my life?" I questioned myself. To be honest, I resented so many obligatory practices. Life affords many opportunities to prepare for marriage, especially in areas of apologizing and resolving conflicts. Let's learn from them for these are skills in which one can *never* be over prepared.

...prepared as a bride beautifully dressed
for her husband.
Revelation 21:2 KJV

"Ditto"

**One doesn't discover new lands without consenting to
lose sight of the shore for a very long time.
Andre Gide**

While reading journal entries sketching a ten-year struggle of my young adult life, I realized, "I could have just put ditto signs after the first entry. *Same* battles, same wounds, *same* tears, *same* fears echoed from the pages year after year after year after year... "Ditto is demonstrated in writing by the " " symbols after whatever came prior. Webster defines the term "ditto" as meaning the *same* as before or another of the *same.*

"*Change* is the only thing that brings *change*" is the lesson I finally grasped. Wishing weeping and whining will not alter our realities. Until willing to embrace new themes and new actions our stories will remain the same— "ditto."

Single life does not have to be *"ditto."* Don't allow it! It can be a transforming pilgrimage of challenge, victory, growth and change! We will never witness real change in our lives unless we dare to launch beyond comfort ranges. Minister Barbara Brown Taylor stated in a sermon, "If I claim one guiding principle for my life, it is to say yes to unusual propositions and see what happens."

Sounds like a worthy challenge! Are you up to it? Plunge into the deep—*with God* and invite Him to charge your life with holy excitement!

**Behold I will do a new thing; now it
shall spring forth' shall ye not know it?
Isaiah 43:19 KJV**

Ifs

**"Whatever you determine to be true in the subconscious
becomes true for you."
Richard Hatch**

Only in retrospect has this phenomenon been unveiled for me. Truth and reality were not deciding factors in relationship choices in the past. Conscious process? Nah— don't think so! This is what I construed while mentally obliterating clear incompatibilities. "Everything will be fine— *i-f*… We can handle those issues *a---nd*... We could get along great— *b--ut*…"

Then presto! A much-improved image of that person featured on my mind's mental screen. Yes! Simply irresistible! Such denial plunged me into an unhappy marriage and a detrimental long-term relationship.

Scenes of pseudo possibilities overrode apparent pitfalls. The results? These self-created illusions left me unearthed and on the brink of mental breakdown. Prodding an unwilling partaker toward their glorified replication existing *only in your head*— is mentally and physically exhausting! Both parties are left totally frustrated. Trust me— the shortcut to insanity is trying to change another person. It will *never* happen! What you see—*is* what you get—for better or worse… and vice versa.

We are packaged deals—once opened the extraordinary— mediocre and objectionable emerge. To enjoy the gift that another has to offer, they must be embraced in their totality. To do this we must be truthful and see *ourselves* and *others* realistically. A companion that I can love and embrace in spite of *real* or *perceived* flaws—no *ifs-ands*-or *buts*— is what I desire—I am *waiting* for him…

**Behold, thou desirest truth in the inward parts…
Psalm 51:6 KJV**

Dabbling

To take a slight and not very serious interest in a subject, or try a particular activity for a short period.
Cambridge Online Dictionary

That dream again! I hated it! It always took a while to reorient myself to reality. In this reoccurring dream I was awakening the morning *after* using crack. I woke up feeling tainted, dazed and remorseful. Once awake, tears formed in my eyes and I thanked the living God that it was *only* a dream. .Mind you, I have never seen, smelled or touched crack. When younger I *dabbled* with marijuana.

Many intelligent people who waited until they have reached their forties or fifties before *dabbling* in drugs; are now struggling for freedom. *Dabbling* has roped people into a debilitating life of drugs as they attempt to eradicate their emotional pain. Over the years my role as a mental health nurse has given me many opportunities to work with those imprisoned by addictions of all sorts including sex, drugs and alcohol. It is only the grace of God that spared me.

God has proven time and time again that he is able to appease the anguish and distressful emotional pain that arise in my life. He is a loving Father who rescued me from a life that could have been severely corrupted by drugs. It doesn't matter if you are *dabbling* or completely *strung out*, you will *never* get in too deep that God's love and grace cannot reach you.

Know ye not that a little leaven leaveneth
the whole lump?
1 Corinthians 5:6 KJV

Recovery

A return to a normal condition.
Online American Heritage Dictionary

Driver's training. A time every teenager looks forward to and many parents dread. I permitted my son to drive short distances during training with me in the car. "You're too close... Slow down a little... Give them more space..." My constant instructions made him feel insecure and he hated it!

Once I felt more comfortable with his increasing skills I seldom offered feedback. One day he made a sharp right turn and failed to straightened the steering wheel quickly enough and hit the curb. . He didn't panic and was back on track in seconds. I was impressed!

I could tell he was bracing himself for criticism. "Good recovery!" I praised. This caught him off guard. "I don't expect you to *never* make driving mistakes, I still make them. What's important is how you respond afterwards."

After receiving salvation we are in discipleship training. God is our instructor. He knows we are going to make mistakes while maneuvering life's highways. He does not write us off when we err. God is more concerned with our corrective measures than our mistakes. When we act wisely by seeking forgiveness, like a proud parent He too is saying *"Good recovery!"*

**If we confess our sins, he is faithful and just
and will forgive us our sins and purify us from all
unrighteousness.
I John 1:9 NIV**

Fantasies

All fantasy should have a solid base in reality.
Max Beerbohm

The dullness of her eyes communicated the sadness in her spirit. Her shoulders slumped from an invisible burden. "Been to any single events lately?" I asked. I met this woman at a single's conference. I'd enjoyed her bubbly persona and humor over the years. Everyone laughed when she shared marital fantasies. Singles tend to create fantasies of marital bliss and file them in the *"perfect marriage"* section of their minds.

She lifted her hand and my eyes sampled the glitter from a petite diamond. "I'm married." She announced with all the excitement of a soldier going off to war while forcing a smile.

"Congratulations!" I gleamed, with genuine joy.

"It was a mistake," her sad voice broke in. "I didn't realize then how good I had it!" She said while sharing some of the difficulties tormenting her marriage to an alcoholic. Her sadness lingered with me like the smell of cigarette smoke trapped in clothing. The blessed event she yearned had become a sentence of doom.

She leapt toward marriage only to have her *happily-ever-after* fantasy dissipate like the mirage of a glistening stream in the midst of a dry, hot desert. There is a gulf between fantasy and reality. If you are not happy and content in a relationship before marriage- don't fool yourself. Marital fantasies will not magically emerge once you say *"I do."*

The eyes of your understanding being enlightened; that
you may know what is the hope of his calling, and what the
riches of the glory of his inheritance in the saints,
Ephesians 1:18

Samaria

The encounter between Jesus and the woman at the well occurs in the region of Samaria in the city of Sychar. Wikianswers.com

The residents of Samaria were lowly esteemed by outsiders and referred to as *"dogs."* Travelers journeyed extra miles to avoid it. Jesus told his disciples that I must go; I *need* to go— to Samaria. You may not be in Samaria heading toward a well in the heat of the day to draw water to care for a man that is not your husband— but many are experiencing their own Samarian experiences. Perhaps your life is infused with guilt and shame. Or maybe it is uncomfortable to be around others because the air is filled with whisperings of the very things you long to forever erase. Samaria is a place where you as well as others are repulsed by your lifestyle - for *whatever* reasons.

If this is you, Jesus is saying that He *"must needs"* go- to meet with *you.* The woman at the well was not seeking Jesus. Yet *He was seeking her.* They initially talked about her singleness— yet she had lived with a succession of men over the years without marriage. Today marriage is disdained by many in our culture and live-in relationships are getting to be the norm.

A series of misfit relationships will siphon your vision, passion and purpose. Those who need Jesus most are often not in the press because they are too *busy* sustaining the status quo of their *miserable* lives. Just one missed beat and like carefully placed rows of dominoes their world would collapse. Like the woman at the well, God loves us and sees the tangled mess our lives become- *without Him.* No matter what the circumstances- Jesus is *always* prepared to meet with you in *your* Samaria.

**And He must needs go through Samaria.
John 4:4 KJV**

Hugs

**We need 4 hugs a day for survival. We need 8 hugs a
day for maintenance. We need 12 hugs
a day for growth."
Virginia Satir**

At a Bishop Jakes' single's conference my eyes
glued on a woman sobbing in agony. "Give her a hug."
This prompting rose inside. The urge increased until I
moved towards her. "Can I give you a hug?" She nodded
and I embraced her. She clung to me while sobbing even
harder.

I am not a huggy person and my arms were soon
ready to release; but "don't let go, don't let go," repeated in
my head. Embracing this stranger was uncomfortable; but
God used my arms to offer His comfort. The force of her
sobs eased and eventually her grip loosened. We smiled,
and turned our focus toward the speaker. I didn't get her
name and would not recognize her today. After that
meeting, it continued happening!

"Give her a hug," those words would grab me
without warning during services. I always asked
permission first. Though it created inner discomfort for me,
it felt great that God was using my arms to reveal the depth
of His love to others. After a couple years I asked, "God,
why doesn't anyone ever give me hug? No big deal, just
curious." That same evening during a service I sat by a
stranger with a beautiful smile. During praise and worship
she looked at me and said, "The Lord wants me to give you
a hug, do you mind?" My heart smiled basking in the
knowledge of my Father's love.

**...we will be able to comfort those who are in any
affliction with the comfort with which we ourselves are
comforted by God.
I Corinthians 1:3,4 KJV**

Epiphany

What is love? Love is when one person knows all of your secrets… your deepest, darkest, most dreadful secrets of which no one else in the world knows… and yet in the end, that one person does not think any less of you; even if the rest of the world   does.
Unknown

"Tell me about yourself." Invitations for self-disclosure- choked me. Words formed in my head but refused to flow through my lips. Embarrassing—I *am* after all an adult! Yet conversations with men has always been difficult. My past is laced with many traumas and this made even general conversation a struggle.

My *epiphany* occurred while reading Dr. John Grays book, "Men are from Mars and Women are from Venus." He wrote about the *healing qualities* of love. He explained that when a person risk exposing past traumas and failures to their partner and this risk is greeted by *unconditional love* and acceptance- healing can occur. It takes *wisdom* to know when to risk being vulnerable and *courage* to do so when the time is right.

I understood this because I could relate it to my salvation. When I repented I felt unbearable shame, guilt and remorse. Each memory of sin and failure that I presented to God, He covered with His love without hesitation. I found liberty in the revelation that this is how it works in relationships. Conversations with men are occurring with increasing ease. Whoever God sends to me will have the grace to cover me with unconditional love *despite* of my past. And by God's grace- I will be able to do the same. .

Most important of all, continue to show deep love for each other, for love covers a multitude of sins.
1 Peter 4:8 NLT

Haters

A person that simply cannot be happy for another person's success. So rather than be happy they make a point of exposing a flaw in that person.
Online Urban Dictionary

I watched a TV talent show with a five million dollar prize. Overconfident contestants taunted and made negative comments about those that they deemed less gifted—before ever witnessing their talents! These teased competitors were already nervous prior to going onstage. Arrogant contestants often gave substandard performances while the ostracized people performances often knocked it out the box!

"You sounded like you were dying!" A judge commented to one contestant after she sung-*poorly*. When denied another chance- she sung again anyways. "Now I feel like I'm dying!" The judge said. When all the judges voted *"no,"* and the more vocal judge concluded, "You sounded annoying." Looking shocked she left the stage with her sister providing much needed support.

Ironically, those marked as certain failures often got standing ovations from the judges, like "You're a superstar! I can see you going all the way!" They stood victorious and vindicated from the wounds of their haters!

The term "hater" is common among the younger generation. Haters are *real!* Preoccupation with them can extinguish the flames of your passions. When pursuing dreams, there will *always* be haters. Pursue your dreams anyways- God has your back. Just like the judges, God will vindicate you in due season- in the presence of your haters.

Thou preparest a table before me
in the presence of my enemies:"
Psalm 23:5

Gilligan

The main character in a popular TV sitcom aired in the sixties.

Gilligan's Island was a hilarious TV sitcom that aired in the sixties. It featured a small group of people that set out on a cruise ship for a three hour tour and ended up stranded on a deserted Island. The comical thing about watching the show was that many times the means for rescue was right in front of them- but they never realized it until it was *too late!*

Some relationships are like this. You go to a bar or maybe the grocery store planning a short excursion. Then a chance encounter ends up being a life changing event lasting years! Hopefully positive; but too often it results in being marooned in a dead end relationship leaving you feeling stranded. It's only in retrospect that rescue efforts by those who care are recognized. Gilligan's Island concluded after three seasons with the cast yet stranded after missing repeated opportunities for escape.

Controlling partners can progressively limit ties with family and friends until your live feels like a desert island. Many are marooned in desert relationships that were doomed from the first kiss.

Some recognize their rescuers and gladly flee to freedom. Others pray for help for years and continually fail to grasp it when it arrives. Emotional ties with others can be made in haste when battling persistent loneliness. It may be difficult to find a way out after investing years of trying to *make it work*. God won't leave you marooned in a dead end relationship. *If* you desire to escape- He *will* rescue you. Will you recognize *His* help when it arrives?

He reached down from heaven and rescued me;
he drew me out of deep waters.
Psalm 18:16 NLT

Original

This is what I learned: that everybody is talented, original and has something important to say.
Brenda Ueland

I want to be a star performer- *for God*. This requires studying my script- *the Bible*. His Word unveils my God-given identity which empowers me to attack my divine role with the utmost confidence. It's sometimes tempting to cloth myself with demeanors observed in others. I resist these urges for God has given me the opportunity to play the role of a lifetime— *myself.*

Each morning I awaken and take the stage of life bringing forth all the gifts, talents and props that God entrusted unto me. The more they're utilized the sharper they become. Others don't always understand my unique approach; but no one can show me how to play *me*. There has *never* been a "me" nor will there ever be another *me.* . My role requires doing and saying things in a manner that only *I* can.

Many chose to play roles seen performed by others because they think it is less risky. Some feel these counterfeit roles make them look more appealing. When God is allowed to direct the course of our lives we open ourselves to infinite possibilities.

There is no failure merely opportunities to reflect, learn and grow. There is nothing more beautiful than an authentic person. God is always happy to find someone who has the courage, strength and faith to play these original scripts, because those who do-*change the world!* Are you willing; are your ready- to just be yourself!

I Am that I Am.
Exodus 3:14 KJV

Write!

**"Writing saved me from the sin and
inconvenience of violence."
Alice Walker**

I encourage journaling because of the emotional benefits. Clarity, insight and direction can all arise from this activity. New ideas like seeds sprouting from a garden can grow into sermons, articles, poems, songs, books, plays, movies- the potential is limitless. Your words can become the source of strength to you or a tool to help others turn tragedy to triumph.

Writing inspired by the Holy Spirit did not end with the Bible. There are many gifted writers some have and others have not learned to assign this gift the respect it deserves. Often writers are afraid to expose themselves as a bonafide writer fearing that *others* will deem them unworthy of this title. Everyone has a story to tell. It takes courage to tell some.

The Holy Spirit has led me to never read books on my shelves for years— to the exact sentence and paragraph needed at a precise moment. The knowledge that someone survived a calamity or overcame hurdles similar to mine was life changing! Your written wisdom may or may not transform into works to be shared with the public.

Instead of taking your unwritten thoughts and ideas to the grave unexpressed- write! Your writing can continue to bring strength and inspiration to you and perhaps others. Written words may continue to speak beyond the grave for centuries to come. Even if it benefits none other than you- it's worth it-*write!*

**And these things write we unto you,
that your joy may be full.
1 John 1:4 KJV**

38

Scales

**Self-delusion is pulling in your stomach
when you step on the scales.
Paul Sweeney**

Stepping off the scale he hid behind an artificial smile while taking his seat. His shoulders fell and a sigh surged the room. "What was your weight today?"

"Oh, I was off the scale." I had never heard this before. I took blood pressures and weights after doctor visits. This young man in his late twenties was with his snooty father and weighed himself as some clients do.

"Yes, you've really blown up!" His father proclaimed with restrained disgust. "You better slow down," he added. I noticed the record for his last weight also read "*off the scale.*" This meant that his weight exceeded the three hundred pound capacity of the office scale.

"Medications can result in rapid weight gain," I defended him to his father. This is true.

"I see how much he packs away. Your mother is going on a diet, I will be joining her and suggest you join us also!" The client visibly trembled at the impact of his father's disapproval. His emotional pain hung in the air as we continued. This is an example of just one person's dilemma with feeling unacceptable because of weight.

Millions plow through this type of rejection daily. God, Our *Heavenly Father* will *never* reject us based on size. His love is steadfast, incomprehensible and is not altered by our weight. We are His creation and regardless of our size the measure of His love for us is *always- off the scale.*

**The Lord hath appeared of old unto me, saying, Yea, I
have loved thee with an everlasting love.
Jeremiah 31:3 KJV**

39

Hypocrite

"Always and never are two words you should always remember never to use."
Wendell Johnson

We are *all* fallible and make mistakes. The problem is when we become arrogant and begin looking down on others as though we were incapable of err. The failures of *others* can become magnified in our minds while ours *seem* microscopic. Over the years I have come to truly appreciate the mercies of God which are renewed daily. Many times I have observed another's imperfections and thought, "I would *never* do that!"

I've done things that I thought *never* do- memories of my disapproving attitude surfaced right after. Like Peter following his denial of the Lord- three times. The cock's screeching left him feeling crushed as he could not imagine *ever* denying Jesus. Peter must have felt- *hypocritical*! The last thing I desire is to live a hypocritical life. I want to be forgiven, embraced and restored when I make mistakes- I am willing to offer the same to others.

Life is a journey marked with victories and defeats, it's great when we get it right; but sometimes we miss the mark. Critical, judgmental attitudes from peers are often what follows when blunders occur. What's needed is the same measure of compassion that we would like to receive if ever found in those very situations. When we magnify the faults of others, our own weaknesses protrude like a facial pimple the size of a watermelon.

You hypocrite, first cast out the beam out of your own eye; and then shall you see clearly to cast out the mote out of your brother's eye.
Matthew 7:5 NLT

Sparkle

Your fear of change is too clearly visible in your eyes"
Douglas Coupland

Looking into the mirror a pair of dull pupils glared back. I was never the most gleeful person, but there was a time when my eyes were illuminated with hope ablazed inside. "God, put back the sparkle in my eyes," I silently prayed. Later that day the scripture below was listed in my devotional reading. I had never noticed it before. David, the author knew how embers of hope could fizzle.

Living alone is only one of the many challenges in a single's life. When facing life's obstacles the desire for a relationship can become last on the list of priorities. There may be battles with layoffs, sickness, financial stressors, family problems, deaths, spiritual issues and the list go on! Often there is no one else to help bear these burdens.

Some singles not only lack a spouse to share the joys and sorrow of life; but family and other supports are *scarce or non-existing.* At times during my journey I had no one- *but God.* Over and over again He has proven to be more than enough. The sparkle in my eyes has dulled during difficult seasons *more than once.* God is a restorer and He is faithful to re-ignite the flames of passion. This resonates inside *"quitting is not an option!"* Hope plunges me closer to my dreams; closer to the manifested promises of God. This hope not only radiates from my heart; but sparkles through my eyes.

Turn and answer me, O LORD my God!
Restore the sparkle to my eyes, or I will die.
Psalms 13:3 NLT

Moments

I glimpse moments left behind me
Where I have failed to act
Some of those opportunities
May never again come back.

I used to feel remorseful
But I'm learning to look ahead
To things that are yet to come
Let bygones be dead!

God is moving by His spirit
His glory to reveal
To a holy vessel
Desiring to do His will.

To take to heights unknown
And pour out His power
To fill with His spirit
And use in this hour.

I shall seize this moment
To glorify His name
For those that trust in Jesus
Shall never be ashamed.

Yes

It is so; as you say or ask. Used to express affirmation, agreement, positive confirmation, or consent
American Heritage Dictionary

Our family cars were clunkers. My father purchased our first *nice* car when I was a senior in high school. My first driver's license was just in time to drive the shiny red convertible. One day I drove my older brother to work and had a tragic. The car was totaled and an elderly man lost his life; I suffered fractured ribs and my younger brother who rode along nose was broken.

My younger sister begged to go and cried when mother said "no." Everyone said she wouldn't have survived when seeing the car's damage. Fear tormented me and I thought I would never drive again. Depression resulted in me leaving school. Facing my father was hard. He never once criticized or made me feel guilty. He was truly thankful that God had spared his children. Sadly, our family reverted to clunkers- *again.*

"Can I drive to the store?" I asked my father about a month later. I braced for his refusal.

"Yes." He replied without hesitation. I sat in the car *amazed.* His eyes glowed with wisdom and love while silently handing me the keys. A denial would have crumbled my confidence and I may have never found the courage to ever drive again. Dad's unconditional love often reminds me of God, my Heavenly Father. Like God, he was willing to look beyond my failures and lavish me with love and forgiveness. God has no checklist of our past mistakes, He is cheering us on to the hope and the future lying ahead. All His promises are, *"Yes."* Trust Him.

For all the promises of God in him are yes, and in him amen, to the glory of God by us.
I Corinthians 1:20

Commitment

Unless commitment is made, there are only promises and hopes... but no plans.
Peter Drucker

I met a guy who was really into fitness and invited me to join a fitness club. I explained that I generally completed what little exercise I did in front of my TV with an instructional video. He called and extended his invitation with special perks for a year – I declined. One time he called and I had actually exercised with my video- three times! I was very proud of myself. My rhythm was soon broken and I was right back in the slump. I shared this short term victory and sudden defeat.

He listened attentively and paused before responding. I thought he was actually empathizing, until he said, "It sounds like a lack of commitment." His voice was kind but; this truth stung. I was no more committed to exercising than walking on stilts. It saddens me; because I *do* want all of the wonderful benefits- I just *don't* want to bother with all that work!

Isn't that the way it is with relationships? Many of us want to enjoy the positive benefits of a *good* relationship; but a *good* relationship doesn't just happen. It takes regular exercises in communication, forgiveness workouts, stretching outside your comfort zone and lots; and lots; and lots…of c-*o-m-m-i-t-m-e-n-t!*

And whatever you do, whether in word or deed, do it all in the name of the Lord Jesus, giving thanks to God the Father through him.
Colossians 3:17 NIV

Overwhelmed

I am overwhelmed.
Fantasia

"God, I'm so overwhelmed, God I'm so…" These words erupted in my mind day and night. Mere words could not expose the depth of my anguish. I had been alone and overly guarded for years. Then I met someone.

"You need to learn to be more trusting," he coached." I prayed, watched and listened-and became more trusting. He was nurturing had an aura of safety. I unveiled my heart and bore my wounds as he poured soothing balm. He invaded a heart space that had been forbidden for years to *all* mankind.

"Finally someone who speaks my language, understands and accepts me for me"- *I thought.* Mutual trust though foreign- was exciting! It felt like I'd tapped into something sacred. Then at warp speed we smashed into an *impasse.* Numbness protected me from the realization — that—it was over! No words expressed the depth of my agony. Not until I discovered the word "invert" which means *"to turn inside out or upside down."* Finally! A description to attach to the emotional distress I endured.

"Speak to me!" I appealed to the Living God.

"Read Psalm 61" were His instructions. I grabbed my bible and fumbled to the scripture below. God reminded me that there was a place with Him that was higher than my pain. A place beyond feelings of regret, loneliness and despair. I could rely on Him to lead me there.

From the end of the earth will I cry unto thee, when my heart is overwhelmed: lead me to the rock that is higher than I.
Psalm 61:2 KJV

Arise

"I am not concerned that you have fallen; I am concerned that you arise."
Abraham Lincoln

Small children zoomed past like pros! My companions glided with ease bouncing to the latest snappy tunes. I envied them. Wobbling around the skating rink with stiff ankles, it was no secret- I was a novice.

One night I *almost* made a complete circle without falling! Though clumsy- it was exhilarating! "Tonight is the night, I will get this!" I wanted to leave a skilled skater; but I plunged to the ground at the *same* curve *every* time.

My rookie efforts drew the attention of a plump school age boy. Leaning against the guardrail he watched. "F-A-L-L!" He yelled- I did.

C-R-A-S-H! I'd plunged to the ground obediently. "Ha-ha-ha!" Irritating laughter filled the air. Then like a voice-controlled pawn each time he'd yell- "F-A-L-L!" at the challenging curve; "P-L-O-P!" I crashed to the floor again and again. I saw no humor after the fourth or fifth time. Yes, I was a tad angry at the kid. A gifted skater I was never to become. I ended my skating career that night- before any permanent disabilities occurred.

Satan, like the mischievous kid finds pleasure in our defeat. He lurks on the sidelines jeering when we fall. He's thrilled when we become discouraged and quit. Life without failure is not realistic. Don't quit! Each time you fall God *will* help you to rise again.

Arise and shine for your light has come and the glory of the Lord has risen upon you.
Isaiah 60:1 KJV

Ask

"If you're not asking for it, you're not going to get it."
Cynthia Schmeiser

"Ask, and you shall receive, seek and you shall find, knock and the door will be opened." These words aired over the radio as I drove to work settling this promise of God into my heart. During lunch I fumbled through the office refrigerator and cabinets searching for jam. I didn't expect to find any, yet I was disappointed. "I wish I had some strawberry jam." I murmured what was meant to be just a futile remark.

"Really? I might have some." A co-worker responded, leaving and returning to the break room with a very *large,* unopened jar of my *favorite* strawberry jam. "Take it home with you," she insisted.

"Wow!" I thought while savoring the taste of my toast and jam. I asked and I received, that simple. Never expected to receive such a large jar of jam- at work! Answered prayer has a way of surfacing at unexpected times and unpredictable manners; but we must ask to get the process started.

God is such a loving Father who takes great pleasure in blessing- us- His children. How many times have I; or have *you* failed to receive because we failed to ask? Selah…

Ask, and it shall be given you; seek, and ye shall find; knock, and it shall be opened unto you:
Matthew 7:7 KJV

Memories

**"Don't cry because it's over.
Smile because it happened."
Dr. Seuss**

Loneliness can result in attachments to others that produce damaging results. I seriously considered marriage to someone- changed my mind and satan *tried* to make me feel like I made a wrong decision. I didn't. We laughed – supported and cared for each other in a way that we both needed during that time. I loved him, in a way that I had never loved anyone before. "Marry me." He asked several times, but I could not move beyond the warning flags billowing between us.

Certain tragedy would have followed had I chosen to proceed. I treasure the surplus of awesome memories of our special moments. He was my friend. It's nice to have people of the opposite sex that you can be yourself with and share laughter- especially when there is mutual respect.

What proves to be a golden friendship can tarnish in the fiery marital trials. Reasons are not always obvious when God issues caution- this is why it is essential to recognize His voice; then trust and obey His guidance. When praying for God's direction during such decisive moments- we don't always get our desired response. It takes strength to walk away from a relationship that is seemingly bursting with promise. God loves us and wants us to understand that all that glitters- *ain't* gold!

**Whether you turn to the right or to the left, your ears
will hear a voice behind you, saying, "This is the way;
walk in it."
Isaiah 30:21 NIV**

Pre-Planned

**The important point is this—to be able at any moment
to sacrifice what we are for what we could become.
Charles DuBois**

Joseph shared his dreams of position, power and
prosperity with eleven brothers Things became chaotic. His
older brother Ruben convinced the others not to kill him;
but they sold him into slavery. Then the wife of his master
falsely accused him of attempted rape. His outraged master
imprisoned him. He had given Joseph special favor and felt
betrayed. Joseph was forgotten by those he aided while
imprisoned and had *promised* to remember him before the
king.

Joseph was single and disconnected from *all* family;
but he submitted to Godly principles instilled in him by his
father since childhood. His integrity and faith sustained him
during these adverse seasons and he chose to forgive. God
caused him to soar above *every* obstacle.

Like a curtain opening for a play's finale; God's
purpose unveiled. Despite all the chaos; Joseph's life was
right on course. Obedience launched Joseph into a position
of power. Joseph married, had children, reunited with
family and saved a nation from famine. What an ending!

Our lives are *preplanned* by God Himself. Every
satanic assignment has been factored in. What *seems*
insurmountable today will work only for our good— when
during seasons of adversity we choose to trust God.

**So do not throw away your confidence; it will be
richly rewarded. You need to persevere so that when
you have done the will of God, you will receive
what he has promised.
Hebrews 10:35 NIV**

Snap!

**Faith is the bird that feels the light and sings
when the dawn is still dark.
Robindranath Tagore**

Lying in bed I wrestled debt, doubt, loneliness, family and financial problems. Worry pinned me to the mattress and I could hardly breathe God ignited a thought inside that continues to navigate me through rough places.

"Snap your fingers." The Lord prompted. Not knowing why- I did. "That's how quickly I can change *any* circumstance in your life!" He reassured me. I smiled and exchanged my anxieties for His peace.

These stressors crept back into my bedroom again threatening to deprive me of sleep. I extended my hand in the air releasing a crisp "snap" into the atmosphere. It's my reminder of the immenseness of God's power. Satan knew exactly what it meant.

I weather many challenges during my pilgrimage as a single woman. God's wisdom doesn't always choose to deliver me instantly, but there's yet peace in knowing that He *can*- in a snap!

**Cast all your anxiety on him because he cares for you.
I Peter 5:7 NIV**

50

Negligent

**Failing to give care or attention, especially
when this causes harm or damage.
MacMillam Online Dictionary**

While driving I glanced into the face of my
innocent seven year old son. "What do you know about
God?" I asked. A blank expression covered his face and I
realized that I was making a grave mistake. His church
exposure was limited to an occasional funeral; God
entrusted me with not only his physical and emotional
wellbeing; but also his spiritual growth-I'd been negligent.

The impact of learning about Jesus during my
childhood was incredible! Growing up presented many
challenges; but I *knew* God was with me. From the age of
eight I began a personal relationship with Him. Though I
got off track, as a young adult, I reconnected. The oldest of
my three children was ten when I left church. Though
young they each had basic spiritual foundation. My broken
relationship with God and the church caused my life to
whirlwind from crisis to crisis. During this dark era my
youngest son was born.

Mesmerized by pain, my child's spiritual needs
never occurred to me. This despondency was robbing him
of an opportunity to know and fellowship with his Creator.
He deserved more! Like many parents in dysfunctional
relationships and troubled marriages or living alone- I was
consumed with surviving. That night was the beginning of
my journey to make sure my son received his spiritual
heritage. Children can experience a void in their lives that
only God can fill. Adults can underestimate the depth of a
child's spiritual hunger. I'm thankful that Jesus *never* does!

**"Suffer little children, and forbid them not, to come
unto me: for of such is the kingdom of heaven."
Matthew 19:14 KJV**

Biscuits

**"If there's always biscuits in the barrel,
where's the fun in biscuits."
Martin Clunes**

When I offer my friendship—I am offering a genuine part of myself. This invitation is only extended when I sense a potential for a positive outcome. It's disappointing when it's belittled and trampled as if worthless—because *more* was desired.

It seems that some men press for *more* in relationships and when not received their friendship is severed- *completely.* "Why are some men reluctant to honor a woman's wish to be "*just* friends?" I was speaking with a man that I met online who was pressing me for more than friendship.

"I can't speak for all men; but for me it's like you *re--ally* like *chicken*—and all someone offers you is a *biscuit!*" We giggled. Though simplistic his explanation opened my understanding of this dilemma—*somewhat.* We continued conversing.

"What are you saying then?" He questioned sensing my unwillingness to move the boundaries of our cordial relationship.

"I guess I'm offering you a *biscuit!*" I said, we laughed. Before long he too dissipated into cyberspace in hot pursuit of *chicken*. Leaving me— again holding a basket filled with the fresh bread of friendship that I was willing to selflessly share.

**They broke bread in their homes and ate
together with glad and sincere hearts.
Acts 2:46 NIV**

Licorice

Means sweet talk in Sanskrit.
holistichealthliving.wordpress.com

I desire to be more outgoing; the hermit's role gets tiring. I want to make some positive connections. So I tried it. I attended a community outdoor event with food and live entertainment. "Hi baby," Similar comments from strange men greeted me as I entered the crowd.

"You leaving already honey?" Such comments followed as I waded through the crowd of people to leave. There are women that feel validated when approached this way. I cringe every time I encounter strangers with licorice. The word licorice means *"sweet talk,"* in Sanskrit. It has always repulsed me when strangers approach me this way- even before I became a Christian.

Sure I want to be called *sugar, honey, baby* someday. Not by someone that flings these words at every warm body that passes, but someone who cares enough to invest quality time into getting to know *me* and values me as a person rather than an impersonal sexual object. Because of the risk of impure motives, we teach children not to take candy from strangers. The same principle applies to adults when it comes to those who lavish *sweet talk.* Beware of licorice.

Let no man deceive you with vain words…
Ephesians 5:6 KJV

Obedience

When I was facing a marital decision as a younger woman, I *strongly* sensed God's disapproval and that He was leading me in the *opposite* direction. Rather than follow His prompting- I got married *anyways*; then prayed that God would overlook my disobedience and make everything alright. I learned that our spiritual journey doesn't work like that and I suffered many negative penalties. What life did I forfeit by choosing my own way? I will never know.

Many years later, while reading the scripture below, a new understanding flooded my mind. "I'm sorry, God. I have been using prayer as a means to order you around. I don't *really* know what I need; I don't always choose what's in my best interest. I surrender to your will." I wept as I prayed asking God to order my steps.

I renewed my commitment to obey God, *whether or not* I liked *or understood* His instructions. Like the children of Israel I have wasted years trusting my own instincts and wandering off the path that God has laid before me. It never succeeds. If we would only walk before God like a child at the mercy of his parents to give guidance and direction - we could avoid much *unnecessary* pain.

**Whether we like it or not, we will obey the LORD our God to whom we are sending you with our plea. For if we obey him, everything will turn out well for us."
Jeremiah 42:6 NLT**

Sweetie

**Those who love deeply never grow old;
they may die of old age, but they die young.
Benjamin Franklin**

Working as a skilled nurse gave me many opportunities to serve people in their homes. One couple stands out in my mind. The woman had infected leg wounds that needed dressings b . She was in a wheelchair and assisted by her husband, who could barely care for himself. They had been married sixty years. Can you imagine? These days some marriages dissolve in less than sixty days. They were adorable. I completed her dressings as they flirted with each other. "Thank you Mr. Sweetie,"

"You are welcome, Mrs. Sweetie." They exchanged these words when he handed her a kleenex. They looked sweet! Love twinkled in their eyes and flowed in the gentleness of their voices. I silently pondered, "God whatever ingredients that are required to still be Mr. and Mrs. Sweetie after sixty years of marriage is worth waiting for- I want it!"

**Pleasant words *are as* a honeycomb, sweet to the soul,
And health to the bones.
Proverbs 16:24 KJV**

Paul

**"That would be kind of an insensitive thing
to do in a situation like that."
Robert Maddox**

While visiting a friend, I sat with her *married* sister
and the topic of singleness emerged. It concluded with her
misquoting Paul in I Corinthians while telling me that it
was better to be single. Frankly, I don't appreciate *married*
couples quoting Paul to illustrate that I'm better off- *single.*
I told her so. This includes pastors and ministers who
magnify this scripture and then in the next breath rave
about their wonderful *marriage*-It's a bit *insensitive.*

Regrettably, a few years later this same woman
became a widow. My heart and prayers went out to her. I
hope that no one quotes Paul's take on singleness to offer
her comfort. If so, she will realize firsthand that this
approach is *not* tactful, I admire Paul and his dedication to
the work of the ministry. Some people are certainly more
gifted than others at living single. Yet God, the Creator of
Paul and the rest of humanity said that, "It is not good for
man to be alone," this goes for women too.

It is vital that as single Christians we strive to reap
as much benefit as possible from this season of our lives. It
is important that we understand and embrace what Paul
wanted us as singles to grasp. It is also key that others,
especially those who are married have the wisdom to know
what circumstances to share this scripture so it will edify
the receiver.

**Like apples of gold in settings of silver is a word
spoken in right circumstances.
Proverbs 25:11 NASB**

Bliss

**The ecstasy of salvation; spiritual joy.
American Heritage Online Dictionary**

Walking through the house my sudden eruptions of praise dismisses the silence. A deep sense of gratitude emerges and joy comes without provocation. I smile because I know I'm having one—a divine moment.

Bliss! That definitive segment of life when my heightened senses perceives—*all* is well. Peace hedges me from the ranting of the universe's chaos – and my imperfect life. The joy of the Lord swells inside me until I am oblivious to all else at that moment—except God's abundant love, grace and mercy.

How I wish times like these were my steady state of being! They are dispersed in healthy doses throughout my pilgrimage. When I'm mindful—I pause to savor each second of these special times.

I love flinging them in satan's face. My thoughts are usually along these lines… "No everything is not perfect; but I believe God is bringing His divine order in my life. Yes it has been years and no… I haven't met anyone special— *yet.*

But I just experienced a divine moment—and you *can't* take that away from me! Just one of such moments compensates for the times that satan has slapped me in the face with frustrations, discouragement, fear and doubt. Victory—such sweet taste—I love it!

**Though you have not seen him, you love him; and even though you do not see him now, you believe in him and are filled with an inexpressible and glorious joy…
I Peter 1:8 NIV**

Bewitched

The devil did not tempt Adam and Eve to steal, to lie, to kill or commit adultery. He tempted them to live independently of God.
Bob Jones Sr.

Charms, candles, roots, herbs, chants and spells—am I still writing about singleness? Yep! Spooky stuff—huh? Tons of books are devoted to *magic* as a means to possess the lover of your dreams! Bookstores are crammed with materials targeting girls before they reach puberty. *Ungodly* tactics are often embraced to explore answers for every arena of life—especially *love* and *romance*.

Spells are offered to find love, keep love, intensify love, drive away-undesired love— and even stabilize roving lovers. When all else fails there are spells to mend your broken heart. Does it work? I've seen and heard some strange stories—the Bible speaks clearly against such practices.

God controls every aspect of the wonders of the universe to its minutest details— yet the decision to love or reject Him was left to our *freewill.* Like my Creator—I desire to be loved— *freely*—because of who I am—no gimmicks, no hocus pocus!

Love is not love when tainted by *manipulation* of another's mind, will or emotions. These are acts of *desperation* by those lacking faith that they are worthy of love and that love will find them any other way. Those indulging in such practices— can *never* know the power, *beauty*, the *power* and *reality* of— *real* love....

"O foolish Galatians, who hath bewitched you, that ye should not obey the truth...
Galatians 3:1 KJV

58

Confabulated

"Such as are your habitual thoughts, such also will be the character of your mind; for the soul is dyed by the thoughts"
Marcus Aurelius

Thoughts of marriage swirled in my head as I awoke. They echoed during church—mid-sermon. This was unusual—honest! My eyes scanned married woman to married woman until they locked onto a certain woman who was nestled smugly against her husband. "Married women should pray more for single women," I decided.

"Ask her to pray for you." A soft prompting rose inside.

"Certainly not!" I silently protested dismissing the thought. "I'll *never* be classified as a *she thinks she is-nothing-without-a-man* woman." I resumed note taking shifting my focus to the sermon. After service I bent to pick up my things and I stood to see that very woman standing by me looking perplexed.

"I'm confused," she began. "I don't even know if you're married; I feel like God wants me pray with you about a husband? Am I missing it?" Baffled, I shared my earlier thoughts. "Marriage isn't always easy," she admitted. But I feel that God is saying that you need someone to come into agreement with you." We joined hands we prayed for each other. I thanked her for her obedience and courage and left church dazed by the amazing way God chose to reveal His love and concern.

O lord, thou hast searched me, and known me.
Thou knowest my downsitting and mine uprising, thou understandest my thought afar off.
Psalm 139:1,2 KJV

Waiting

I'm waiting for him
He's seeking for me…
I trust in God's word
And what shall be shall be…

Each day as I strive
To walk in God's will…
My heart's desire
Shall be fulfilled…

A person to share
My dreams, hopes & life…
Uniting as one
As husband & wife…

Until then I'll flourish
And grow in God's grace…
By seeking His purpose
By seeking His face…

Who? When? Where?
I do not know
But in the fullness of time
It shall be so…

Live!

He who has a why to live can bear almost any how.
Friedrich Nietzsche

She threatens to kill herself every time I try to leave this relationship. I have wanted to get out of it for a long time! I took her to the emergency room and filed forms to have her committed." Variations on this story are common on psychiatric units from males and females. For some suicide is a threat and others it is a fatal completed act.

A man shared news about a teenager's suicide. He was a fifteen year old son of a friend who lived in another state. "He taped a picture of his ex-girlfriend to his chest and killed himself!" This teen died senselessly in the name of— *love*. Love was never meant to be destructive!

Often when asking suicidal people, "How long have you been in this relationship?" Frequently the response is a few months or even less- this is baffling. Whether it's a day or twenty years feelings of anxiety, hopelessness and abandonment experienced makes moving on without *that* particular person *seem* impossible. Physical and emotional attachment to another person resulting in that person becoming vital to your existence is neither healthy nor wise. This level of dependency is best reserved for God alone.

Over the course of our lives people will come and go. God alone is able to fulfill the promise to *never* leave. God will give you strength to forge ahead - even when you feel like you can't. If you are battling suicidal thoughts; this day *profess* to yourself *I can,* I *will,* l-i-v-e!

I shall not die, but live, and declare
the works of the LORD.
Psalm 118:17 KJV

Greedy

"The riskiest thing you can do is get greedy."
Lance Armstrong

A client introduced me to a game called *"Greedy."* This game is played by computing the numbers after each roll of die. The first one that reaches the score of 100 wins. The object is to accumulate points without rolling the number "one." Once the number one is rolled the points already tabulated are secure; but all points for that turn are forfeited.

"I can always feel when I am going to roll a "one," she said while rolling the die. "See! I knew it was coming!" The rolling die landed with the "one" side upwards. It was my turn. I had accumulated 38 points and felt that I should stop. Dismissing the internal warning I rolled once more. Sure enough the number "one" flaunted itself at me.

"I knew I should have stopped!" I laughed. I won the game- but not until I disciplined myself to *stop* rolling the die when my inner sensor directed. This game is an excellent metaphor of how the Holy Spirits operates. He is faithful to warn when peril is ahead. Greed results in consequences that can not only be painful but long-lasting. Whether confronted by lust of the eye, flesh or pride- just like the game, greed can result in severe loss rather than gain.

"But God said to him, 'You fool! This very night your life will be demanded from you. Then who will get what you have prepared for yourself?' "This is how it will be with anyone who stores up things for himself but is not rich toward God."
Luke 12:20, 21 NIV

Dreams

"In imagination, there's no limitation."
Mark victor Hansen

"When I grow up, I'm going to build me a house..." Desmond, my then seven year old son declared. This was followed by elaborate details about his imagined future dwelling. "Then I am going to build you a house-- right next door..." this was followed by exquisite specifications of every minute feature of my fantasy home.

Growing up in a family with skimpy finances- My dreams were shrunk to death by disillusionment. This gave birth to the *"don't-expect-too-much-from-life* mindset rooted in poverty. I decided to spare him disappointment by paring his fantasies to more realistic portions. "No!" I sensed God warning. "I gave him those dreams- don't destroy them!"

I reflected on the early dreams of my childhood trampled by adults with good intentions attempting to spare me future frustration. Thank God for His intervention.

My son has grown into a fine young man. "Mom, take this to church for me," he said handing me money for his tithes before leaving for work. Though he has not acquired millionaire status- *yet;* he has emerged into adulthood with his dreams intact. I cannot wait to see what God does in his life! I'm starting to do a little dreaming again myself.

Perhaps you are a single parent. Years of struggle and sacrifice can result in discouragement and the dismantling of dreams. Allow God to rekindle your dormant dreams. After all- it *could* happen...

When the Lord restored the fortunes of Zion, we were like those who dreamed. Our mouths were filled with laughter, our tongues with songs of joy.
Psalm 126:1,2 NIV

Kisses...

Never let a fool kiss you, or a kiss fool you...
Joey Adams

"Kiss"— to touch or press with the lips as a sign of love, affection, passion, or respect." (Wordnik) Some kisses are disloyal. A friend shared how she was lead to salvation. "He was an *attractive, single, Christian* man. It was hard for him *not* to kiss me, because—*"I'm a stump-down-good-lookin-woman!"* I giggled. Though she was flirtatious she appreciates how *he* focused on witnessing. "I was at a crossroad and considering becoming a Muslim and prayed, "God if You show me that You're real, I will serve you. God *sent* this man to show me the way."

"Just *one* kiss!" I taunted, trying to seduce him! His passion for God rose above sexual desires. "He did not betray me with a kiss." She said grateful in retrospect. "Had he responded to my advances, I'd *never* have taken him seriously." This woman is now one of the most effective soul winners I know personally.

Many have been snatched from eternal damnation because a man refused distraction and stood for his beliefs. Singles are effective with winning other singles to Christ- *if* they stay focused. Tainting witnessing with lust betrays not only God, but ourselves and the person God is attempting to reach- through us. Perhaps you are ministering to someone God is preparing for another. When the response is sexual overtones- stay focused. Just imagine, right now- in another city, state or country someone may be ministering to the person God created specifically for you.

Judas, betrayest thou the son of man with a kiss?
Luke 22:48 KJV

Vengeance

Infliction of punishment in return for a wrong committed; retribution.
Online American Heritage Dictionary

Ever ran into a brick wall in an automobile going 100 mph? Well that's what getting dumped in a relationship can feel like- hence the term *"emotional wreck."* The funny thing is, even if you are dumped by a person you were planning on dumping- *it still hurts*. A part of you pray they will return- so you will have the opportunity to exit *first* -next time.

A man was suing on a court TV reality show. A couple lived together and had a young child- he left; *without warning*. The woman was devastated. They made amends and even resumed their relationship. Then the woman left- *without warning.* Only she took *everything* including his bed and sold it! She admitted feeling vindicated. Sadly, amidst these alternating break-ups was an innocent child. Break ups are not easy for anyone.

Those who have accepted Jesus have become the sons and daughter of God. The Bible teaches us how to treat each other to avoid causing each other undue emotional distress. Unfortunately, we don't always grasp or apply biblical practices and we hurt each other- *intentionally.* Whether pain is caused *intentional* or *unintentional* life becomes a bitter journey if wasted on simply seeking vengeance.

Dearly beloved, avenge not yourselves, but rather give place unto wrath: for it is written, Vengeance is mine; I will repay, says the Lord.
Romans 12:19 KJV

Taken

"Having possession gained especially by force or effort."
Online Wordnet

The movie, *Taken* depicts a daughter that took a trip with a friend to Italy without telling her father. Not long after arriving both girls were abducted by human traffickers. The daughter watched through a window while her friend was dragged out of the house. Hiding under the bed she phoned her father on a cell phone.

"They are going to take you," using those few seconds to impart instruction, strength and hope. "*I promise* that I will come for you," He said. The father was a man of special skills and strong political connections. In Hollywood fashion, he rescued his daughter even after she had been handed over to the highest bidder and was headed to an unknown destination.

I sighed thinking what it would be like to have a father who would fight for me to that end! God immediately refreshed my mind and I recalled the numerous times He and the Heavenly Host waged spiritual warfare to retrieve me from satan's grasp. I repented recognizing that I *do* have a Father who loves me dearly and is willing to do *anything* for me. Let's take a moment to lift up those in prayer that are snared by the diabolical market of human trafficking.

At that time I will gather you; at that time I will bring you home. I will give you honor and praise among all the peoples of the earth when I restore your fortunes before your very eyes," says the LORD.
Zephaniah 3:20 NIV

Confidence

**To thy own self be true for only then canst thou be true
to any other man.**
Shakespeare

"I dreamt that I was walking through a store's
parking lot- nude. A man approached me from behind and
pinched my bottom. Seething with righteous indignation I
turned abruptly and slapped his face. I kept walking as
though being naked in broad daylight was perfectly natural.

"What do you think it means?" I questioned a friend
that was gifted with interpreting dreams.

"What emotions were you feeling?"

"My posture was really erect, I felt so at ease."

"I think it means that you are starting to feel more
comfortable with yourself." This made sense. Working on
increasing both my confidence and self-esteem were
priorities then. After wrestling feelings of failure and poor
self-esteem for years I dared to face them head on. Looking
into the mirror each day I repeated affirmations.

The positive words about me from my own lips
made me laugh at first. I internalized them over time and
the process of learning to love and value myself began. The
reward was that my opinion of me now outweighed that of
others.

Months earlier I was attired in threads of guilt and
shame. Though not literally like the dream, I have the
boldness to expose my authentic self to the world. Despite
faults, mistakes and physical flaws I am okay. I'm
discovering the freedom to love myself and others.

Love thy neighbor as thyself.
Matthew 22:39 NIV

Smart

A man must be big enough to admit his mistakes, smart enough to profit from them, and strong enough to correct them.
John C. Maxwell

"You never remarried?"

"No," I said.

"You're smart!" I attended church with this woman years ago when we were both much younger. Our paths crossed and we spent time accounting for previous years.

"I would like to." I quickly clarified.

"I was just divorced a year ago, she continued. We were together for thirteen years; then married for eighteen."

Then I understood her stance; *pain* was speaking. When my long term relationship ended; it was several years before I considered opening my heart again. "I still believe in marriage and I believe that there are many good marriages and I believe that *I* can have one." I said.

I thought about what she said. It made me realize that I am *smart*. Smart enough to not allow fear to rob me of future possibilities. Smart enough to move beyond the dread that the past will repeat itself. Smart enough to learn from past mistakes and keep moving forward. Like life, love offers no guarantees but I am smart enough to know that marriage is a risk and can be well worth it.

But since sexual immorality is occurring, each man should have sexual relations with his own wife, and each woman with her own husband.
I Corinthians 7:2 NIV

Warnings

Dreams are the answers to questions that we haven't yet figured out how to ask."
Fox Mulder

Baffled, I awoke from a dream. In it I find myself lying in bed next to my husband- a man God rescued me from years ago. Surging with mixed emotions I wondered "How did I get here? At the same time I was questioning, "What can '*I* 'do to make this work?"

The answer *was* then and *is* now *"nothing."* Thank God, some things are just *not* meant to be. "Why has this dream resurfaced over the past ten years?" I pondered while shivering and shaking off the hebegebies. The scripture in Job below helped me to realize that it's God's merciful way of warning me.

Sometimes the only thing new about our relationships is the outer packaging. We find ourselves face to face with the same destructive issues from the past.

I'm taking this warning serious and noting the things that pronounced doom in previous situations. I'm not talking about a checklist to compare everyone I meet with him. Certain things need to reside in forefront of the mind to avoid replication. Once I understood this that dream never returned.

God forbid that someday I look at the husband lying beside me whom I have awaited for so-ooo long— only to discover—it's him! Someone I barely escaped years ago. I pray for discernment and ask God to cause me to recognize those with seeds of potential for a positive outcome of a sacred union...I'm waiting for him...

God speaks again and again though people do not recognize it. He speaks in dreams, in visions of the night when deep sleep falls on people as they be in bed.
Job 33:14, 15

69

Greener

**"If the grass is greener on the other side of the fence,
you can bet the water bill is higher"**
Anonymous

We can spend our lives admiring other people lawns or take time to nurture our own.

My daughter said, "I was looking at the neighbor's grass and it looked so green and beautiful *compared* to ours. Then when I was further down the street I looked at ours and it looked just as green as the neighbors." Sometimes couples look at the lives of singles and singles look at the lives of couples and each can *seem* to have greener lawns/lives.

But a well-tended lawn/live whether married or single can actually be quite beautiful. Singleness is a time when God is fertilizing the soil of our hearts and cultivating dormant gifts and talents. If we are receptive to the Holy Spirit's teaching and pruning during these times- when a marriage partner arrives- we will be better equipped for this new season.

Some married couple's lives have become dried, brown and overcome by weeds. Growth is stunted in their marriage because they are no longer watering their relationship with words of life. Whose grass is greener is a matter of perspective. In the end it doesn't matter whose lawn is greener- but whether or not you are content with the lawn you have. Whether married or single, God can cause our lives to be vibrant and blossom. All it takes is the seed of His Word, the rain of His Spirit and the light of His Son to nurture our lives on a regular basis.

He maketh me to lie down in green pastures:
He leadeth me beside the still waters.
Psalms 23:2 KJV

Puzzle

In our finiteness we must continually drop to our faces before God in worship, saying, I bow before you as one of your creatures. Thank you that while I cannot understand everything, my hand is held by the eternal, all wise, Infinite God, the Creator.
Edith Schaffer

Life mirrors an incomplete puzzle. Me—as a finished product is ever before God. He works— *knowing* where each piece belongs and inserts them with care at *appointed* times.

"Ouch! Don't think this one fits!" I've complained when a newly inserted segment resulted in discomfort. I've attempted to assist God *many* times by inserting *things*, *relationships*; *circumstances* that inwardly, I *knew* didn't belong in my life.

My interferences only intensify my discomfort and I *run* to God (*again*) for answers. Stripping away my counterfeit efforts He patiently continues— preoccupied with perfecting me.

Sure that next interlocking unit could manifest the man of my dreams! But— what if the puzzle is completed—and there is *no* man? Will I still stand firm on a foundation of faith? Or will I become angry, disillusioned and bitter?

I have come to trust that God's options are *always* best. I'm confident that He will *never* abandon His work (me). Selah…. I cling to God's promises while submitting my life to Him— the Master Puzzler.

Trust in the LORD with all your heart and lean not on your own understanding; in all your ways acknowledge him, and he will make your paths straight.
Proverbs 3:5, 6 NIV

Why?

Here we are, trapped in the amber of the moment.
There is no why.
Kurt Vonnegut

"Why are you *s-t-i-l-l* single?" When asked this question -*I cringed.* Have you noticed that the same people tend to ask year after year? There are many reasons a person may be *s-t-i-l-l* single. Some have not been approached by *suitable* partners. Some have not been approached at all. Some have decided they would say *"no"* regardless of who approaches. Some are healing from a traumatizing past and simply are *not ready* to reopen their hearts…and the list goes on.

There is no reason for me- or you to defend singleness- to *anyone*. It's not some defect that demands explanation. It is not a disease that can spread. It is not a flaw nor a crime punishable by law!

The single journey is personal, challenging and unique. For some it is a brief phase. For others it's a lingering season stretching over many years. And for some it becomes a permanent lifestyle. Singles may not want to expound or issue routine explanations to those unable to empathize.

The challenges of this journey are demanding enough without trying to appease the curiosity of others. I no longer do that song and dance; I love God, He loves me; I'm, single- so what? I'm yet about my Father's business. Isn't that what's most important?

That is why, for Christ's sake, I delight in weaknesses,
in insults, in hardships, in persecutions, in difficulties.
For when I am weak, then I am strong.
2 Corinthians 2:10 NIV

Answers...

**I have learned to place myself before God everyday
as a vessel to be filled with His Holy Spirit.
Andrew Murray**

The ambience of the restaurant induced relaxation. Laughter mingled with muffled conversations and soft music filtered the air. It was our church's annual fashion show. "What is the first flower to bloom in spring?" The Mistress of Ceremony was having a trivia and rewarding prizes for correct responses.

"Roses!"

"Nope!"

"Tulips!

"No, that's not it!"

"Lilies!

"Aren't there any green thumbs in here!" the MC chuckled refuting each incorrect response.

I sat clueless and exasperated from mentally straining to conjure up something. I know zip about flowers. "Holy Spirit you are the Spirit of Truth and know all things," What is the answer?"

"Sorry, no one got that one! Let's try another question. The answer is... "

"*M A G N O L I A S*" The correct answer was softly laid in my mind precisely when spoken by the MC. I knew the Holy Spirit had responded to my simplistic prayer-- I would never had offered that response.

"Wow!" The Holy Spirit is committed to *lead* and *guide* us into *all* truth. Whether trivia, relationships or life's most perplexing situations- God has *all* the answers.

**Howbeit when He the Spirit of Truth, is
come, He shall guide you into all truth...
St. John 16:13 KJV**

Seeking

While seeking the will
Of my Father above
He's leading me to
An everlasting love…

She's out there somewhere
And someday I'll find
A loving companion
That I can call mine…

Her breathtaking beauty
Radiating from within…
My wife, my lover
My very best friend…

She's out there somewhere
Though many faces I see…
I'm searching for the one
God ordained just for me…

Who? When? Where?
I do not know
But in the fullness of time
It shall be so…

A Prayer for You...

Father, I pray that your strength, comfort and peace will flow into the lives of my single brothers and sisters who may or may not be reading this book. Go before them and make all their crooked places straight. Lead to repentance unto salvation anyone that has not experienced the beauty of being adopted by You.

I pray that You, Holy Spirit will strengthen, counsel, teach and keep those who are living single and trusting in You for wisdom and guidance. Direct men and women to their path that will aid in accelerating the fulfillment of their divine purpose and destiny. I pray that they will each experience the ultimate reward of salvation— in order to live hereafter eternally in Your presence.

I pray that you meet every need in this reader's life according to your riches in glory. Impart spiritual discernment along with a willing and obedient spirit that satanic pitfalls may be avoided and demonic assignments cancelled.

Father, I pray that you will quiet the voice of the enemy whispering deceitful lies into the ears of those single Christians desiring to serve you. Let God arise and His enemies be scattered! Let them hear your voice clearly. Strengthen them with might by your Spirit in their inner man. I pray that you sustain and keep them while granting the desires of their hearts.

In Jesus Name,
Amen

Therefore,

do not throw away your

confidence, which has a great

reward. For you have need of

endurance, so that when you have

done the will of God, you may

receive what was promised.

For yet in a very little while, He

who is coming will come, and will

not delay.

Hebrews 10:35-37 NASB

About the Author

Jeri Darby is a registered nurse with over 25 years' experience working with those receiving mental health treatment. She currently works with seniors. Jeri has ministered to men and women in jail, prison, halfway houses and shelters. Jeri served as president for both the Women's Weekend Retreat Outreach Ministry and Seeking and Waiting Singles Ministry which she was also founder. She is currently president of Aglow Int'l-Saginaw Lighthouse which is part of an International ministry committed to restoring others to a radiant place of light. She has been requested to lead a single's ministry at her local church.

Jeri has spoken at single's conferences and written and directed plays addressing issues related to singles. She is a freelance writer and the story of how she began her nursing career has been published in 'Chicken Soup for the Nurse's Soul a Second Dose' (*Crisis Bridge*). There are over 100 publishing credits for her articles and poems appearing in Decision, Evangel, Women of Spirit, Upper Room, Women Alive!, Joyful Woman, Lookout, Standard, Righteous Nurse, Pentecostal Evangel, Purpose and others.

Jeri is currently writing *Stepping Stones-Reflections for Singles Volume II.* Jeri has a vision to launch a ministry focused on healing and restoration between mothers, daughters and granddaughters experiencing the pain of broken relationships. She embraces the reality that she is the King's Daughter and lives a life of surrender and service to her Father, God.

Watch for more books by Jeri Darby on Amazon.com. You can contact Jeri at araritypress@gmail.com.

Thank you for purchasing my first book.

Stepping Stones
Reflections for Singles
Volume I

If you have enjoyed this edition; watch for

Stepping Stones
Volume II

And other forthcoming books by Jeri Darby at:
Amazon.com
&
Kindle